ROMANIA TRAVEL GUIDE 2023

Ultimate Guide Book To Romania 2023

By

Annie C. Priest

Table Of Content

Chapter 1. Introduction

Map of Romania

Welcome to Romania, a nation with a fascinating history, breathtaking natural scenery, and a fascinating fusion of cultures. Romania is a country in Southeast Europe. Romania has plenty to offer any traveller, from the rough peaks of the Carpathian Mountains to the lovely ancient cities. Romania offers a wide range of activities, like seeing historic castles, dining on delectable regional fare, and immersing yourself in lively customs.

Travellers to Romania will find a wide variety of regions, each with an own personality. Although Transylvania is likely the most well-known part of the nation due to its Gothic architecture and eerie folklore, there is so much more to see outside of its boundaries. Romania is brimming with surprises, from the Maramures' verdant woods to the Danube Delta's status as a UNESCO World Heritage Site.

The sights, cultural experiences, and natural wonders of Romania will be highlighted in this travel guide as we take you on a tour of the region. This book will provide you with all the knowledge you need to make the most of your time in Romania, regardless of whether you're planning a quick vacation or a longer stay. So gather your belongings and get ready for a memorable journey in this captivating region of Europe.

Tip #1: Brief overview of Romania as a travel destination

Dava, HD, Romania

Situated in Southeast Europe, Romania is a nation renowned for its breathtaking natural scenery, intriguing past, and distinctive culture. Romania provides a wide variety of outdoor activities, including hiking, skiing, and swimming, from the snow-capped Carpathian Mountains to the unspoiled Black Sea beaches.

Several historic sites can be found throughout the nation, notably Bran Castle, which is frequently linked to the Dracula legend, and the Transylvanian mediaeval castles. History aficionados also like visiting Sighisoara, a fortified city and the birthplace of Vlad the Impaler.

A blend of Romanian, Hungarian, and German influences make up the rich and diversified cultural heritage of Romania, which is in addition to its natural beauty and historical landmarks. In Romania's capital, Bucharest, visitors may take in traditional music and dance performances, eat local fare, and discover a thriving street art culture.

Visitors to Romania will discover welcoming hosts and cosy lodgings in a range of locations, from beautiful guest houses in the countryside to opulent hotels in the capital.

Tip #2: Important things to know before travelling to Romania

When visiting Romania, make sure to keep the following in mind:

Visa requirements: You could need a visa to enter Romania depending on your nationality. During stays up to 90 days, people from the United States, Canada, the European Union, and many other nations are not required to get a visa to enter

Romania. For the latest information, contact the Romanian embassy in your nation.

Language: Although English is widely spoken, especially in tourist hotspots, Romanian is the country's official language. To facilitate communication with locals, it's always a good idea to learn a few fundamental Romanian words and phrases.

The Romanian leu is the country's unit of exchange (RON). Credit cards are readily accepted everywhere, especially in cities, and ATMs are widely available.

Romania is a relatively safe country, however it is always advisable to exercise caution wherever you go. In crowded places, keep an eye on your belongings, and stay off the streets at night when you're alone.

Transportation: In Romania, especially in bigger cities like Bucharest, public transit is both inexpensive and effective. Taxis are also easily accessible, however choose trustworthy providers and bargain the rate before boarding the vehicle.

Winters are frigid and summers are hot in Romania, which has four distinct seasons. Before leaving, check the weather forecast and pack appropriately.

Food: Romanian food is substantial and savoury, with influences from nearby nations like Serbia and Hungary. Foods like sarmale (stuffed cabbage rolls) and mici are deserving of your attention (grilled minced meat rolls).

Culture and history: The ancient Roman and Byzantine empires, as well as the more recent communist era, have all left their marks on Romania's rich cultural and historical heritage. See historic sites including the Palace of the Parliament and Bran Castle.

Nature & outdoor pursuits: The Carpathian Mountains and the Danube Delta are just two examples of Romania's breathtaking natural splendour. Activities for outdoor enthusiasts include hiking, skiing, and river rafting.

Etiquette: Although Romanians are typically amiable and welcoming, it's vital to be aware of regional customs and social protocol. For instance, it's considered disrespectful to visit someone's home without bringing a small present (such a box of chocolates or a bottle of wine).

Tip #3: Useful travel tips for visitors

Tourists who want to experience Romania's distinct charm frequently travel there. Here are some helpful travel advice to assist you have a successful vacation, whether you're visiting Romania for the first time or are an experienced traveller:

Learn about the local currency – The Romanian Leu is the currency used there (RON). When visiting rural areas in particular, be sure to carry some cash with you because certain establishments might not accept credit cards.

Although English is often spoken in tourist regions, it is always a good idea to learn some fundamental Romanian words. This will improve your ability to interact with locals and demonstrate your appreciation for their way of life.

Romania has a variety of temperatures, so it's necessary to pack adequately. It can get rather hot during the summer, so pack light, comfortable attire. Pack warm clothes and shoes because winter temperatures might drop drastically.

Be cautious when using a cab − In Romania, taxis are typically secure, but beware of frauds. Always check to see if the taxi has a working metre. Before boarding, seek a price estimate from a local or the front desk of your hotel if you're unclear about the fee.

Taste some of the local cuisine; it's wonderful and diverse. Try traditional foods like sarmale (stuffed cabbage rolls), mici (grilled minced beef buns), and ciorba without hesitation (a sour soup).

Respect religious sites; there are many stunning churches and monasteries in Romania. When visiting these locations, remember to dress modestly and show consideration for anyone who is engaged in worship or prayer.

Explore the countryside; there are several little villages and towns to discover in Romania's breathtakingly beautiful countryside. A fantastic approach to explore the nation at your own leisure is to rent a car or work with a guide.

Pickpockets should be avoided − Romania, like every tourist destination, has its fair share of pickpockets. Keep an eye on your possessions, particularly when using public transportation or in crowded settings.

Keep yourself hydrated because it can get extremely hot in Romania throughout the summer. Have a water bottle on you at all times, and be sure to refill it.

Make travel arrangements in advance; Romania hosts a number of festivals and events throughout the year. For instance, the Sibiu International Theatre Festival takes place in June and July, as does the Bucharest International Film Festival.

Chapter 2. Pre Trip Planning

If you are planning a trip to Romania, there are several things you should keep in mind before you go.

Tip #4: What To Pack

The following is a list of things you should carry for your vacation to Romania:

When going to Romania, especially for non-EU nationals, you must have your passport or other form of identification with you at all times.

Visa: Make sure to have your visa on hand if you need one to enter Romania.

Save a copy of your vacation itinerary, which should include your hotel reservations and flight information.

The Romanian leu is the country's official currency (RON). Carry cash with you or use your credit card to get cash from ATMs.

Clothing: There are four distinct seasons in Romania, so prepare appropriately. Winters might be cold, so bring heavy jackets and boots, and summers can be hot, so light clothes are advised.

Pack appropriate shoes for sightseeing in Romania because there are many lovely walking routes there.

Bring amenities like toothpaste, shampoo, soap, and sunscreen, as well as your toothbrush.

Medication: If you need to bring any medication, remember to do so.

Camera: There are many breathtaking vistas and sceneries in Romania, so make sure to bring yours.

Guidebook: A guidebook might be useful for learning about the history and culture of Romania.

Having a language translation app can be useful because Romanian is the country's official language and not everyone speaks English.

Tip #5: Accessories

The following is a list of possible travel accessories for Romania:

Travel adapter: Because Romania utilises the Europlug type C electrical socket, you will need one to charge your gadgets if you are travelling from a nation that uses a different type of plug.

Portable Charger: If you intend to spend a lot of time trekking in the Carpathian Mountains or discovering Romania's natural splendour, a portable charger can keep your phone charged in case of emergencies.

Whether you're planning a day trip or a multi-day journey, a comfortable and durable backpack might be crucial while seeing Romania. Get one that can hold your necessities, such as water bottles, food, and a rain jacket.

Water bottle: It's important to stay hydrated, especially in the summer heat. You may save money by not purchasing single-use plastic water bottles and stay hydrated all day long with the aid of a reusable water bottle.

Wearable Shoes: Romania can be difficult on your feet due to its cobblestone streets, mountainous landscape, and hiking paths. Pack a pair of comfy shoes that are appropriate for the activities you intend to perform, whether they involve sightseeing, hiking, or just general city exploration.

Travel Pillow and Blanket: Whether you're travelling to Romania via long flight or train, a travel cushion and blanket can keep you cosy and allow you to rest.

First Aid Kit: In the event of minor illnesses or injuries, a first aid kit can be quite helpful. Bring supplies like pain relievers, bandages, antiseptic cream, and any necessary prescription drugs.

Pack sunscreen with a high SPF and some sunglasses to cut down on glare to protect yourself from the sun's damaging rays.

Having a guidebook or map can be useful for navigating new areas in Romania and learning about new locations, whether you prefer classic paper maps or digital maps on your phone.

Tip #6: Men Outerwear

The following is a list of men's outerwear to bring to Romania:

Winter Coat - A warm and reliable winter coat is necessary if you're travelling in the winter.

Pack a waterproof rain jacket because Romania has frequent showers of precipitation all year round.

Lightweight Jacket - For chilly days when a bulky coat is unnecessary, a lightweight jacket is ideal.

Bring a fleece or sweater to wear under your jacket because layering is the key to staying warm in Romania.

Wearing a scarf, hat, and gloves will keep you warm and cosy throughout the chilly weather.

Hiking Footwear - A reliable pair of hiking boots is required if you intend to engage in any outdoor activities.

Sneakers - A pair of cushy sneakers is ideal for commuting through cities and villages.

Swim Trunks - If you're travelling during the summer, remember to bring swim trunks so you can enjoy the beaches and pools.

Convertible Pants - These trousers have a simple conversion process that allows them to be worn as shorts in a variety of climates.

Windbreaker - A windbreaker can be layered over a sweater or fleece for additional warmth and is perfect for windy days.

Tip #7: Women Outerwear

The following is a list of women's outerwear goods to think about bringing on your vacation to Romania:

You may want to pack a larger coat or a lighter jacket depending on the time of year you're visiting. A thick, insulated coat will be required during the winter months, while a lighter jacket may be adequate during the warmer months.

Raincoat or umbrella - Rainfall is often in Romania, especially in the spring and summer, so having a raincoat or an umbrella on hand can be helpful.

Scarf: A scarf is a multipurpose piece of clothing that may both keep you warm and add colour to your look.

Hat - In the winter months, a hat helps keep your head and ears warm. In the summer, it can shield you from the sun.

Gloves can keep your hands warm and shielded from the cold during the winter.

Cardigan or sweater - On chilly days, a cardigan or sweater is a terrific layering option that can keep you warm.

Fleece or hoodie - You can layer additional outerwear items over a fleece or hoodie to create a comfy and casual look.

Boots - Especially in the winter, comfortable, waterproof boots are a need for negotiating Romania's occasionally slick and rainy streets.

Tip #8: Men Footwear

The following is a list of men's shoes to bring to Romania:

Walking shoes that are comfortable to wear are essential because many of Romania's historic cities have uneven sidewalks and cobblestone streets.

Hiking boots are a need if you intend to travel across Romania's mountainous regions. On rocky terrain, they give your feet support and stability.

Sandals are an excellent alternative for keeping your feet cool and comfy because it can get rather warm in Romania during the summer.

Dress shoes - It's a good idea to bring a pair of dress shoes if you intend to go to any formal events or upscale restaurants.

Rain boots are a smart idea to pack because Romania can suffer significant rainfall, especially in the spring and fall.

Sneakers are perfect for casual occasions and can be used for jogging or light workout.

Flip-flops are a practical and simple-to-pack solution if you intend to visit any beaches or go swimming.

Slippers: While slippers for indoor usage may be provided by certain hotels in Romania, it's always a good idea to bring along a pair for comfort and hygienic reasons.

Winter boots - If you're planning a trip to Romania in the dead of winter, make sure to bring some toasty, insulated boots to keep your feet warm and dry.

Tip #9: Women Footwear

The following list of women's shoes may be useful to bring for your trip to Romania:

Pack a pair of comfy shoes that are appropriate for lengthy walks because Romania offers many chances for walking, from exploring towns to mountaineering in the mountains.

Sandals: If you intend to spend time outdoors or visit the beach during the summer months, a pair of comfy sandals might be a terrific investment.

Dress shoes: You might wish to carry a pair of dress shoes to go with your attire if you have any formal events or fancy dinner plans.

Rain boots: Depending on the season you're travelling during, rain boots can make a terrific addition to your luggage. If you encounter rainy conditions, they will keep your feet dry and cosy.

Boots for hiking: If you intend to go trekking or exploring in the mountains, you must have a reliable pair of hiking boots. Ensure that they are cozy and offer your feet the support they need.

Sneakers: Sneakers are a flexible alternative for both exercising and walking. They might be utilised for exercise or simply as a cosy solution for city exploration.

Flip flops: If you plan on wandering around your hotel or relaxing by the pool, a pair of flip flops can be a fantastic choice.

Tip #10: Toiletries

The following is a list of toiletries that you might want to carry for your vacation to Romania:

Brush and toothpaste: It's crucial to practise proper dental hygiene at all times, but especially when travelling.

Shampoo and condition :are essential for maintaining healthy hair in Romania because of the region-specific temperature variations.

Body wash or soap: They are necessary for daily cleansing and hygiene.

Deodorant: It's crucial to stay fresh in warm weather or after a full day of activities.

Razor and shaving cream: It is imperative for men who shave to have a razor and shaving cream.

Sunscreen: It's crucial to protect your skin from the sun, especially in the summer.

Insect repellent: As Romania contains mosquitoes and other insects, it is a good idea to bring insect repellent.

Hand sanitizer: With the pandemic still going strong, it's always a good idea to have hand sanitizer.

Feminine hygiene items: It's crucial for ladies to bring any necessary feminine hygiene items.

Moisturiser: Your skin may become dry depending on the climate, so bringing a moisturiser might help keep it nourished.

It's crucial to take the weather and your planned activities into account when packing toiletries for a trip to Romania. Aside from that, if you're staying in a hotel, you might already have basic essentials like soap and shampoo, so make sure to ask before you pack.

Chapter 3. Getting To Romania

Braso, BV, Romania

Depending on where you're coming from and what kind of transportation you like best, there are a number of ways to reach Romania.

Tip #11: Transportation options for getting to Romania

Worldwide travellers are choosing Romania as a vacation location more frequently. There are a variety of ways to go to Romania, whether you're going there on business or for fun. In this post, we'll examine some of the most popular choices and offer some advice on how to pick the one that will meet your needs the best.

Travel by Air

Air travel is one of the most common ways to reach Romania. Several international airports serve the nation, the largest and busiest of which is Bucharest Henri Coanda International Airport. Other significant airports in România include Timișoara Traian Vuia International Airport, Iasi International Airport, and Cluj-Napoca International Airport.

Many airlines offer flights to Romania, including well-known airlines like Turkish Airlines, Air France, Delta, and Air France. To go to Romania, you might need to take one or more connecting flights, depending on where you're coming from.

To receive the best deals, it's crucial to book your flights far in advance if you're planning to fly to Romania. To receive benefits for your travel, you might also want to think about signing up for a frequent flyer program.

Travel by Rail

Train travel to Romania is an additional alternative. Trains run often over international borders to connect Romania with other European nations including Austria, Germany, and Hungary.

CFR Calatori, which runs both local and foreign trains, is the principal train operator in Romania. Depending on your budget and travel requirements, there are various types of tickets available on Romania's trains, which are often spotless and pleasant.

One benefit of taking the train is being able to take in the countryside, which can be very lovely in Romania. Train travel can be slower than flying, and you might need to change trains numerous times to get where you're going.

Travel by Bus

Bus travel can be a fantastic alternative if you're seeking a cheap way to get to Romania. Many international bus companies, such as Flixbus and Eurolines, run trips to Romania from other European nations.

Bus travel can be more flexible than air or train travel because there are frequently more departures and arrivals, which is one of its benefits.

Furthermore, certain bus routes offer nighttime service, which can enable you to reduce your lodging expenses.

Bus travel can, however, also be slower and less comfortable for longer trips than air or train travel. You can also encounter some hiccups because Romanian roads can be difficult, especially in rural areas.

Travel by Car

Renting a car can be a smart alternative if you want to explore Romania while you're there. This will allow you the freedom to travel at your own leisure and might be especially helpful if you intend to visit remote locations or tiny towns.

Hertz, Avis, and Europcar are just a few of the worldwide automobile rental firms that are active in Romania. Driving in Romania, however, can be difficult, especially in bigger cities like Bucharest, which can be chaotic and congested.

Furthermore, certain of Romania's roads, particularly those in rural areas, can be in poor shape, so it's necessary to drive carefully. It's important to keep in mind that drinking and driving is illegal in Romania, therefore refraining from it is imperative if you intend to drive.

Making the Best Decision

It's crucial to take your travel requirements, tastes, and financial situation into account while selecting a mode of transportation to get to Romania. For instance, plane travel can be the ideal alternative if you're seeking a quick and handy option. Yet, if you're on a tight budget, using the bus or train can be a better option.

It's crucial to take your trip schedule into account. Renting a car might be a wise decision if you have many places in Romania on your itinerary. Yet, public transportation can be a more economical choice if you're only visiting one or two locations.

Researching the numerous transportation alternatives and businesses that are available to you is also crucial. This can aid in locating the greatest offers and ensuring that the company you are using for your trip is credible.

Finally, it's important to note that Romania is a relatively safe country to visit and that most Romanians are hospitable and friendly to travellers. But, it's crucial to exercise standard safety procedures, such as avoiding dark, lonely areas at night, protecting your belongings, and being alert of your surroundings.

Tip #12: Visa requirements and other entry regulations

Understanding the visa requirements and entry requirements is crucial if you're planning a trip to Romania in order to avoid any problems.

Romanian visa regulations

Depending on your nationality, the reason for your trip, and how long you plan to stay, you may need a visa to enter Romania. Visa-free entry is available to citizens of Switzerland, the European Union (EU), and the European Economic Area (EEA). They are permitted to remain in Romania for a maximum of 90 days throughout the course of six months. They must, however, have a current passport or ID card, and if they intend to stay in Romania for more than 90 days, they must register with the Romanian Immigration Service.

Romanian entry may require a visa if you are a citizen of a nation outside the EU/EEA/Switzerland. Your visit's purpose will determine what kind of visa you require. Visas come in many different forms, including transit, business, and tourist visas. The most popular type of tourist visa is the short-stay (type C) visa, which permits you to stay in Romania for up to 90 days over the course of six months. You must apply for a long-stay visa if you want to stay more than 90 days (type D).

You must apply for a visa at a Romanian embassy or consulate in your country of residence. A valid passport, a completed visa application form, and additional supporting documents, such as a hotel reservation confirmation, a travel schedule, and proof of your ability to sustain yourself financially during your stay, are required. A criminal background check and a medical certificate may also be required.

Depending on the amount of applications at the embassy or consulate and your nationality, the processing period for a Romanian visa can change. You should apply for your visa well in advance of the date you intend to go in order to prevent any delays.

Romanian entry requirements

While visiting Romania, there are additional entry criteria in addition to the visa requirements that you should be aware of. They comprise:

Validity of Passport: Your passport must be valid for at least six months beyond the expected length of your visit to Romania.

Border Control: You will go through border control when you arrive in Romania. A passport check, a visa check (if necessary), and inquiries about the reason for your visit may be part of this process.

Customs Rules: You are permitted to enter Romania with duty-free personal effects, including clothing, electronics, and mementos. the Romanian embassy or consulate in your country should be contacted if you have any questions concerning the customs policies.

Romania does not have any restrictions on the amount of currency visitors may bring in. The customs officials must be notified if you are carrying more than 10,000 euros (or the equivalent in another currency).

Rules pertaining to health: There are no particular health requirements for entry into Romania. Nonetheless, you might be asked to present documentation of your immunizations or a medical certificate if you are coming from a place where there is a significant risk of infectious diseases.

Tip #13: Tips for navigating Romania's airports and train stations

Navigating Romania's airports and train terminals can be difficult for travellers, especially if you are unfamiliar with the country's public transit system. We will offer you advice in this article to make it easier for you to manoeuvre around Romania's airports and train stations.

Guide to Airport Navigation in Romania

Consider your options for transportation, your departure and arrival times, and other details before you leave for the airport. You may escape the last-minute rush by doing this, which will guarantee that you get to the airport in plenty of time.

Before you get to the airport, check the flight schedule to make sure there haven't been any changes to the time of your flight's departure or arrival. Before heading to the airport, you can also check the flight status online.

Security screenings are a crucial component of airport travel, so be prepared for them. Make sure you are ready by taking off your shoes, removing any metal objects from your pockets, and putting your electronic gadgets in a different tray. This will help the process go more quickly.

Choosing the Correct Terminal: Several airports have more than one terminal, so it's important to know which one you need to go to. To find out which terminal to go to, visit your airline's website or get in touch with them.

Learn the Layout of the Airport: As soon as you get to the airport, take some time to become comfortable with the layout, which includes knowing where the check-in counters, boarding gates, and amenities like restaurants and restrooms are.

Utilise Public Transportation: If you're on a tight budget, think about taking the public transit to and from the airport. It is frequently less expensive to take a bus or rail from the majority of airports than to take a taxi to the city centre.

Booking a Taxi: If you decide to use a cab, make sure to do so through a trustworthy business to prevent fraud. Ask about the fee before boarding a cab at the stand, which is often outside the terminal.

Suggestions for Getting Around Romania's Rail Stations

Plan Your Route: Choose your route, including your departure and arrival times as well as the train you'll be using, before you go to the train station. Online or at the station, you can also purchase your ticket in advance.

Verify the Train Schedule: As soon as you get to the station, check the train schedule to make sure that there haven't been any alterations to the departure or arrival times for your train. In addition, before heading to the station, you can check the status of the train online.

Decide on a Platform: It's critical to know which platform your train will leave from in order to navigate crowded train stations. The station employees can be contacted for assistance or you can check the electronic display boards.

Purchase Your Ticket: If you haven't done so already, you can do it at the station's ticket window or using the self-service kiosks. Don't forget to bring cash or a credit card.

The best way to prepare for security inspections at train stations is to take out any metal objects from your pockets and put your electronic devices in a different bag.

Railroad stations can be crowded, so it's important to take precautions to protect your possessions. Avoid leaving your bags unattended and keep your passport, wallet, and other valuables near to you.

Utilise Public Transit: If you're travelling on a tight budget, think about taking public transit to and from the train station. It is frequently less expensive to take a bus or tram from the majority of train stations than to take a taxi to the city centre.

Chapter 4. Regions And Cities

Situated in southeast Europe, Romania shares borders with Ukraine, Moldova, Hungary, Serbia, and Bulgaria. Bucharest, the nation's capital and largest city, is one of 42 counties that make up this region.

Romania's regions are divided into four geographical areas:

1.The Carpathian Mountains
2. The Transylvanian Plateau
3. The Moldavian Plateau
4. The Wallachian Plain.

These regions are home to a variety of cities, each with their own unique history, culture, and architecture.

1.The Carpathian Mountains

The beautiful range of peaks and valleys known as the Romanian Carpathian Mountains spans most of central and eastern Europe. The Carpathians play a significant role in the geography and history of

Romania because of its exquisite natural beauty, distinctive culture, and profusion of animals.

Over 1,500 kilometres, from the Czech Republic in the north to Romania in the south, the Carpathian Mountains form a crescent-shaped mountain range. Nearly a third of Romania is covered by the Carpathians, a mountain range that separates the nation into Moldavia in the east, Transylvania in the west, and Wallachia in the south. The Fagaras Mountains' Moldoveanu Peak, with a height of 2,544 metres, is the highest point in Romania.

The Carpathians are renowned for their varied topography, which features lofty peaks, deep valleys, and a variety of marshes, grasslands, and woods. Along with approximately 3,000 plant species, the mountains are home to a variety of animals and plants, including bears, wolves, lynx, wild boar, and deer. With countless rivers and streams winding through the mountains and supplying millions of people with irrigation water and drinking water, the Carpathians are a significant source of water for the area as well.

The rich cultural heritage of the Carpathians is one of its most distinctive features. For thousands of years, several ethnic groups have lived in the highlands, and each group has left its stamp on the history and culture of the area. The Carpathians have a long and illustrious history with the Romanian people, including several traditions and rituals that have been handed down through the decades. In addition, the area is home to a number of minority groups, including the Roma, who have their own unique culture and traditions.

The Carpathians are well-liked among outdoor enthusiasts in addition to tourists interested in nature and culture. Rock climbing, mountain biking, skiing, and hiking are just a few of the sports available in the mountains. Additionally, the area is home to a sizable number of spas and wellness facilities, which provide a variety of therapies and treatments aimed at enhancing health and wellbeing.

The village of Sinaia, which is situated in the Bucegi Mountains, is one of the Carpathians' most well-liked tourist sites. The Peles Castle, a magnificent palace constructed in the late 19th century for the Romanian royal family, is one of Nasa's most notable features. Sinaia is also noted for its beautiful surroundings and rich history.

Brasov, a town in Transylvania, is another well-known tourist destination in the Carpathians. Brasov is renowned for its elegant old buildings, quaint cobblestone streets, and thriving cultural scene. Visitors to Brasov have a variety of options, including visiting the city's several museums and art galleries, riding a cable car to the summit of Mt. Tampa for sweeping views of the area, or visiting Bran Castle, which is close by and is thought to be the source of the Dracula legend.

2. The Transylvanian Plateau

In the heart of Romania, there lies a sizable plateau known as the Transylvanian Plateau. It is surrounded by the Southern Carpathians to the south, the Apuseni Mountains to the west, and the Carpathian Mountains to the east, covering an area of roughly 100,000 square kilometres. With sporadic volcanic outcrops, the plateau is primarily composed of sedimentary rocks.

With elevations ranging from 200 to 500 metres above sea level, the Transylvanian Plateau offers a varied landscape. It is scattered with numerous hills, valleys, and plains, making it the perfect place for farming. Coal, salt, and oil are only a few of the abundant mineral resources in the area.

The Transylvanian Plateau has a continental climate with chilly winters and mild summers. The area experiences moderate annual rainfall, with the spring and summer being the wettest seasons. Fog is another problem on the plateau, particularly in the fall and winter.

A wide variety of plants and fauna can be found on the plateau. Deciduous trees including oak, beech, and hornbeam make up the majority of the region's woods. Numerous bird species, including owls, hawks, and eagles, can be seen on the plateau. Fish of many types, including trout and carp, can be found in the rivers and streams of the area.

The Transylvanian Plateau has a lengthy history and vibrant culture. There is historical evidence of human habitation in the area that dates back to the

Paleolithic epoch. The plateau was a key place for trade and cultivation throughout the Roman Empire.

The plateau was governed by a number of Romanian principalities and kingdoms during the Middle Ages. Numerous ethnic groups, including Saxons, Hungarians, and Roma, also called the area home. The architecture, cuisine, and customs of the area still reflect this rich cultural legacy.

The city of Sighisoara is one of the Transylvanian Plateau's most important historical sites. One of the best-preserved mediaeval towns in Europe is Sighisoara, which is perched on a hill above the Tarnava Mare River. The Clock Tower, the Church on the Hill, and the Venetian House are just a few of the city's many historic structures and sites.

The fortified church of Biertan is a noteworthy feature on the Transylvanian Plateau. One of the most significant specimens of Transylvanian Saxon architecture is the church, which was constructed in the 15th century. The church is especially renowned for its imposing defence walls and fortified towers.

The traditional food of the Transylvanian Plateau is very well renowned. The cuisine of the area is a combination of Saxon, Hungarian, and Romanian influences. Sarmale (stuffed cabbage rolls), goulash, and kurtos kalacs (a sort of sweet pastry) are also well-liked foods. Numerous vineyards that produce some of Romania's best wines are located on the plateau.

The Transylvanian Plateau has grown in popularity as a tourist attraction recently. Visitors from all over the world have been drawn to the area by its natural beauty, extensive history, and distinctive culture. Visitors can take part in a variety of outdoor activities, such as hiking, cycling, and skiing, as well as discover the area's various historic sites and delectable cuisine.

3. The Moldavian Plateau

The Moldavian Plateau, often referred to as the Moldavian Platform or the Moldavian Plain, is a sizable geographical formation that can be found in the northeastern region of Romania. The Prut River and the Carpathian Mountains both encircle the plateau, which has a surface area of about 41,000 square kilometres. The Moldavian Plateau, one of Romania's most significant agricultural regions, is distinguished by its rolling hills, rich soils, and temperate temperature.

Geologically speaking, the Moldavian Plateau is a component of the greater East European Craton, a stable, old block of continental crust that has largely escaped the effects of tectonic action for billions of years. Sandstones, shales, and limestones, among other sedimentary rocks, were deposited on the plateau during the Paleozoic and Mesozoic eras. Over time, these rocks were worn, creating the distinctive undulating hills and wide valleys that characterise the area.

Numerous plant and animal species can be found on the Moldavian Plateau, including riparian habitats, grasslands, wetlands, and oak and beech forests. The golden eagle, the black stork, and the lesser spotted eagle are just a few of the bird species that use the plateau as an important breeding habitat. A number of rare and endangered animals, including the European bison, Carpathian lynx, and European otter, also call this area home.

One of the most significant agricultural areas in Romania is the Moldavian Plateau, which cultivates a range of crops, including wheat, corn, barley, sunflowers, and grapes. In addition to producing wine, the area is also well-known for producing honey, dairy products, and other agricultural products on a small scale utilising age-old techniques.

The Moldavian Plateau has a long history of human habitation that dates back to the Palaeolithic era.

Before becoming a part of the Kingdom of Romania in 1918, the area was later occupied by Dacians, Romans, and several nomadic tribes. The area has historically been shaped by a number of cultures, including Byzantine, Ottoman, and Austro-Hungarian.

Numerous significant historical and cultural sites may be found on the Moldavian Plateau today. The painted monasteries of Bucovina, a UNESCO World Heritage site that consists of eight monasteries embellished with frescoes that date back to the 15th and 16th centuries, is among the most noteworthy. The monasteries are renowned for their vivid hues and elaborate decorations, which feature themes from the Bible and saints' lives.

The city of Iasi, which was Romania's cultural and intellectual hub in the nineteenth century, is another significant location in the area. The Metropolitan Cathedral, the Palace of Culture, and the Vasile Alecsandri National Theater are just a few of the city's notable landmarks.

The Moldavian Plateau, as a whole, is an intriguing region that provides an insight into the rich history and culture of Romania. With its undulating hills, rich soils, and varied flora and fauna, it is an essential component of the nation's agricultural industry, and its historical and cultural sites bear witness to the region's ongoing legacy.

4. The Wallachian Plain

A physical and historic region in Romania is the Wallachian Plain, sometimes referred to as Muntenia. It is situated in the southern region of the nation, between the Carpathian Mountains and the Danube River, and it has a total size of almost 44,000 square kilometres. The Wallachian Plain is a significant agricultural region in Romania as well as a hub for commerce and tourism.

The Wallachian Plain's history dates back to the prehistoric era, when numerous tribes and kingdoms lived there. Of these, the Dacians, who fought the Roman Empire in the first and second century AD, are the most well-known. In the future, the area joined the Byzantine Empire, then the Bulgarian Empire, and in the late 19th century, the Kingdom of Romania.

Flat, fertile land and a temperate climate are characteristics of the Wallachian Plain. Numerous significant rivers that provide water for irrigation and transportation, including the Olt, Arges, and Dambovita, pass the area. A number of lakes, including Lake Snagov and Lake Caldararu, can be found on the Wallachian Plain and are popular tourist destinations.

Bucharest, the capital of Romania, is one of the most significant cities in the Wallachian Plain. There are many museums, theatres, and universities in Bucharest, a significant cultural and economic hub. The Palace of the Parliament, one of the biggest buildings in the world, and other notable architectural works in the city are well known.

Pitesti, a major city in the Wallachian Plain and a centre of the auto industry, is another significant city. The Automobile Dacia factory is located in Pitesti and creates automobiles for both the domestic and international markets in Romania. A number of universities and technical colleges can be found in the city, which is also a major hub for education.

With meals like sarmale (stuffed cabbage rolls), mici (grilled minced beef rolls), and ciorba (a sour soup prepared with vegetables and pork), the Wallachian Plain is renowned for its traditional cuisine. Also well-known are the wines produced in the area, particularly the red wines made in the Dealu Mare vineyards.

Visitors can enjoy a number of sights on the Wallachian Plain, a well-liked tourist site. Bran Castle, one of the most well-known, is thought to have served as the model for Dracula by Bram Stoker. It is possible to visit the castle year-round, and it is close to the city of Brasov. The Snagov Monastery, Peles Castle, and the Danube Delta are a few additional well-liked tourist attractions on the Wallachian Plain.

The Wallachian Plain is notable for its historical and cultural landmarks, in addition to being a significant hub for business and industry. In addition to fruits like apples and plums, the area also produces a wide range of crops, such as wheat, corn, and sunflowers. In addition, there are a number of enterprises and industrial parks on the Wallachian Plain that manufacture everything from electronics to textiles.

Tip #14: Overview of Romania's different regions

Travellers find Romania to be a fascinating destination because of its diverse regions' unique cultures, histories, and landscapes. A summary of Romania's many regions will be given in this page.

Dobrogea

A region called Dobrogea, which borders the Black Sea, is situated in the southeast of Romania. Sand beaches, ecological preserves, and historical sites are all prominent features of the area. With over 300 different bird species living there, the Danube Delta in Dobrogea—a UNESCO World Heritage Site—is a birdwatcher's delight. The Histria Fortress and the Roman city of Tomis are two further ancient Greek and Roman ruins found in the area.

Banat

Horse racing in banat Romania

On Romania's western border with Serbia and Hungary is the region of Banat. A large number of Germans, Serbs, and Hungarians live in the area, which is renowned for its multicultural past. The Semenic-Cheile Caraşului National Park and the Danube Gorge are two of the region's many environmental preserves and national parks.

Maramures

In the north of Romania, close to the Ukrainian border, is the region of Maramures. The area is renowned for its traditional way of life, which includes festivals, wooden homes and churches, traditional clothing, and traditional accessories. A number of natural wonders may also be found in the area, such as the Merry Cemetery, a peculiar cemetery where the gravestones are adorned with vibrant and amusing artwork.

Oltenia

With borders to Serbia and Bulgaria, Oltenia is a region in the southwest of Romania. The Cozia National Park and the Olt River Gorges are only two examples of the area's stunning natural features. Additionally, there are a number of historical monuments in the area, such as the Horezu Monastery, which is listed as a UNESCO World Heritage Site and is well-known for its exquisite ceramics and murals.

Tip #15: Guide to Romania's major cities, including Bucharest, Cluj-Napoca, and Timişoara

Romania is a stunning nation in Southeast Europe that is bordered by the countries of Ukraine, Moldova, Bulgaria, Serbia, and Hungary. Its big cities are brimming with charm and personality, and its history and culture are rich. In this guide, we'll look at three of Romania's most well-known cities: Timişoara, Cluj-Napoca, and Bucharest.

Bucharest

With a population of more than 2 million, Bucharest is both the capital and largest city of Romania. A bustling metropolis, it combines both old-world allure and contemporary conveniences. Numerous museums, parks, historical sites, and nightlife hotspots can be found throughout the city. Top tourist destinations in Bucharest include:

After the Pentagon, this enormous structure known as the Palace of the Parliament is the world's second-largest administrative structure. It was constructed by former Romanian dictator Nicolae Ceaușescu, and it presently serves as the location of the country's legislative body.

The Old Town of Bucharest is the city's historic core and is home to a labyrinth of winding lanes, quaint shops, and historic structures. It's a fantastic location for exploring and getting a sense of the city.

Village Museum: Located throughout Romania, this outdoor museum displays traditional homes, churches, and other structures. It's an excellent site to study Romanian history and culture.

Herastrau Park is Bucharest's biggest park and features a lake, trails for walking, and a lot of open space. Picnics, jogging, and relaxation are all common activities there.

Cluj-Napoca

With a population of more than 400,000, Cluj-Napoca is the second-largest city in România. It is in the centre of Transylvania and renowned for its thriving cultural scene and youthful vitality. Top tourist destinations in Cluj-Napoca include:

One of Cluj-Napoca's most recognizable monuments is the Gothic St. Michael's Church. It was constructed in the fourteenth century and has a magnificent bell tower as well as beautiful brickwork.

The Cluj-Napoca Botanical Garden is one of Romania's largest botanical gardens, with more than 10,000 different plant varieties. A fantastic area to unwind and take in the scenery.

Walking routes, play areas, and a lake can be found in Cluj-Napoca's Central Park, which is a public space. Both residents and tourists like visiting this location.

The National Museum of Transylvanian History is a museum that chronicles Transylvania's history and culture from prehistoric times to the present. It's an excellent spot to discover the lengthy history of the area.

Timişoara

With a population of more than 300,000, Timişoara is the third-largest city in România. It is situated in the country's western region, close to the borders with Serbia and Hungary. It has a distinguished architectural style, a diverse population, and a thriving arts community. Timişoara's major attractions include the following:

Timişoara's central area, Union area, is flanked by opulent structures, cafes, and stores. It's an excellent spot for people-watching and relaxation.

One of the city's most recognizable landmarks is the magnificent Timişoara Orthodox Cathedral.

Beautiful stained glass windows and frescoes can be found there.

Victory Square is the location of the Timişoara National Theatre and a statue of Romania's King Ferdinand I. You may find some of the city's most stunning buildings there.

One of Timişoara's oldest and best-preserved attractions is the mediaeval fortress known as Huniade, which dates back to the 14th century. It's a wonderful site to discover the city's history and admire its stunning architecture.

Timişoara Art Museum: This gallery exhibits paintings, sculptures, and ceramics made in Romania and elsewhere. You may learn a lot about the local art scene and find new artists there.

Other Romanian cities that are worth a visit

There are many additional cities in Romania that are worth seeing in addition to the most well-known ones, Bucharest, Cluj-Napoca, and Timişoara. Here are a few of these:

Brasov: In the centre of Transylvania, this gorgeous mediaeval city is renowned for its beautiful architecture and quaint old town.

Sibiu: Sibiu is a stunning mediaeval city in Transylvania that is well-known for its historical landmarks and cultural attractions.

Known for its stunning beaches and historic sites, like the former Roman city of Tomis, Constanta is a Black Sea coastal city.

Iasi: This city in northern Romania is renowned for its stunning architecture and thriving arts scene.

Tip #16: Suggestions for off-the-beaten-path destinations to visit

Even if some of Romania's most well-known locations, including Bucharest, Brasov, and Transylvania, are worthwhile to visit, there are also a lot of off-the-beaten-path locations that provide an exceptional and genuine travel experience. Here are some ideas for places to go that are off the beaten path in Romania.

Sinaia – Often referred to as the "Pearl of the Carpathians," Sinaia is a picturesque mountain resort town situated in the Prahova Valley, in the heart of the Carpathian Mountains. It is the location of the magnificent Peles Castle, one of Europe's most beautiful castles, and the Monastery of Sinaia, a must-see for anybody interested in religious architecture.

Corvin Castle is a Gothic-Renaissance castle that was built in the 14th century and is situated in the western region of Romania. It is often referred to as Hunyadi Castle. With a lengthy history and intriguing mythology surrounding it, it is one of Europe's biggest and most spectacular castles. For everyone who enjoys both history and architecture, it is a must-visit location.

Danube Delta - The Danube Delta is one of the largest and most beautiful wetlands in the world, as well as one of Europe. More than 5,000 different plant and animal species, including endangered ones like the European mink, Danube Delta horse, and white-tailed eagle, can be found there. It is a haven for those who enjoy the outdoors, birdwatching, and wildlife.

Maramures is a region in northern Romania that is renowned for its traditional rural lifestyle, wooden churches, and distinctive customs and traditions. It is a fantastic place to visit if you want to learn about real Romanian culture and lifestyle. Maramures also contains the Merry Cemetery in Sapanta, a peculiar graveyard well known for its vibrant gravestones and amusing epitaphs.

Known for its towers, defensive walls, and cobblestone lanes, Sighisoara is a tiny mediaeval settlement in the centre of Transylvania. It is a terrific spot to visit whether you're interested in history, architecture, or vampire lore because it is where Vlad Tepes, better known as Dracula, was born.

Alba Iulia: is a historic city in central Romania that is well-known for its spectacular citadel, one of the biggest and best-preserved Vauban-style fortresses in all of Europe. It also serves as the location of the National Museum of Unification, which tells the tale of Romania's 1918 unification.

Known for its fortified church, which is a UNESCO World Heritage Site, Biertan is a tiny village in Transylvania. The church is surrounded by towers and reinforced walls, and it has a special lock system that permits divorcing couples to be imprisoned in a room for two weeks while making an effort to patch things up.

Targu Jiu: is a small town in southern Romania that is well-known for the magnificent sculptures that were created there by Constantin Brancusi, one of the most well-known artists in the country. Anyone interested in sculpture or art must visit the sculptures, which are situated in a lovely park and include the Endless Column, the Gate of the Kiss, and the Table of Silence.Known for its painted monasteries, which are now UNESCO World Heritage Sites, Bucovina is a region in the northeastern section of Romania. The bright frescoes that decorate the painted monasteries, such as Voronet, Humor, and Moldovita, show scenes from the Bible and the lives of saints. They are evidence of the talent and originality of the old Romanian painters and craftspeople.

Transfagarasan Highway - The Transfagarasan Highway winds through the Fagaras Mountains in central Romania and is one of the most breathtaking mountain highways in the world. Anyone who enjoys driving, hiking, and taking in the gorgeous mountain scenery should visit here. Due to the extensive snowfall throughout the winter, the road is only accessible from June to October.

The Bicaz Gorges are a magnificent natural landmark in the Eastern Carpathians famed for its soaring cliffs, raging river, and breathtaking scenery. They make for fantastic hiking, rock climbing, and nature excursions.

Retezat National Park - Situated in the Southern Carpathians, Retezat National Park is one of Romania's most stunning and biologically varied national parks. Over 1,000 different kinds of flora and animals call it home, including rare and imperilled ones like the brown bear, lynx, and chamois. It's a wonderful location for hiking, wildlife viewing, and taking in the beautiful views.

Apuseni Mountains - The Apuseni Mountains are a stunning mountain range in western Romania that is yet mostly unexplored. They are well-known for their magnificent caves, including the Bears' Cave and the Scarisoara Ice Cave, as well as their traditional rural lifestyle and distinctive culture.

Calafat - Calafat is a tiny city in the southern region of Romania and is well-known for its magnificent Danube Bridge, which links Romania and Bulgaria. For those who enjoy engineering and design, the bridge—the longest and most contemporary on the Danube—is a wonderful vacation spot.

Cluj-Napoca – Known for its rich cultural diversity, bustling art scene, and exciting nightlife, Cluj-Napoca is a thriving and dynamic city in the heart of Transylvania. It also has a thriving tech sector, a sizable student population, and numerous museums, galleries, theatres, and festivals.

Chapter 5. Accommodations

From affordable hostels and guesthouses to opulent hotels and resorts, Romania offers a variety of lodging options.

Tip #17: Overview of different types of accommodations in Romania

There are various different types of lodgings accessible for travellers to Romania:

Hotels: In Romania, hotels are among the most often used forms of lodging. The bigger cities, such Bucharest, Cluj-Napoca, and Timişoara, have a number of high-end hotels that provide first-rate amenities and services. These hotels frequently provide fine restaurants, spa services, workout facilities, and swimming pools. In addition, the nation is home to a number of midrange and inexpensive hotels. These lodgings are ideal for travellers on a limited budget who nevertheless want a decent place to stay.

Guesthouses: Guesthouses are another well-liked lodging choice in Romania. Guesthouses give guests a chance to experience the local culture and way of life because they are frequently found in smaller towns and villages. Many inns are run and owned by families, and visitors are given family-like treatment. Traditional Romanian cuisine is frequently given to visitors, and many guest houses provide activities like horseback riding and hiking.

Hostels: Hostels are an excellent choice for tourists on a tight budget. Hostels can be found all over Romania, notably in the bigger towns like Bucharest and Cluj-Napoca. Dorm-style lodging is available at hostels, which are also great places to meet other travellers. It is simple for visitors to socialise at hostels because many of them provide common facilities like kitchens, lounges, and outdoor spaces.

Airbnb: Over the past few years, Airbnb has grown in popularity in Romania. Visitors have the option of renting a complete apartment, home, or just one particular room. Airbnb gives visitors the chance to live like a local and frequently offers a more genuine experience than booking lodging at a hotel. Additionally, especially for bigger parties, Airbnb may be less expensive than conventional lodging.

Camping: In Romania, camping is a fantastic alternative for individuals who love the outdoors. There are several campgrounds in the nation, many of them are situated in breathtaking natural settings. Camping is a wonderful opportunity to explore Romania's breathtaking countryside up close and can be a cost-effective lodging option.

Resorts: Romania boasts a number of resorts spread out over the nation for those seeking a more opulent experience. A lot of resorts are situated in scenic locales like the Carpathian Mountains or the Black Sea coast. In resorts, visitors can unwind and unwind while taking in the breathtaking surroundings. Numerous resorts include great dining options, spa facilities, and a variety of outdoor activities.

Pensions: Pensions are comparable to guesthouses, except they are frequently found in cities. Visitors are treated like family in these establishments, which are frequently run by families. While still enjoying hotel amenities like private bathrooms and air conditioning, pensions give visitors an opportunity to get a taste of the local culture and way of life.

Tip #18: Tips for finding the best hotels, hostels, and other lodging options

Finding the best hotels, hostels, and other lodging alternatives in Romania can be difficult, especially if you're unfamiliar with the country. Here are some pointers to help you locate the best housing options in Romania.

Research is the first step in locating the best housing options in Romania. Look for different hotels, hostels, and other lodging alternatives online and read reviews left by past visitors. To find hotels and hostels in Romania, use travel search engines like TripAdvisor or Expedia. To obtain a sense of the calibre of the services and amenities provided, make sure you read the reviews and ratings attentively.

Location: Take into account the location when selecting a hotel, hostel, or other type of lodging.

Select a hotel that is close to the sights or locations you intend to see. It will be simpler for you to navigate the city if there are taxis or public transportation nearby.

The hotel, hostel, or other lodging option's amenities are crucial. Make sure to confirm whether the hotel has extras like free Wi-Fi, air conditioning, and a full breakfast. Additionally, some hotels could provide extra services like laundry, an airport shuttle, and spa treatments. Choose a solution that meets your demands and budget after taking into account the amenities provided.

Budget: It's important to adhere to a budget when travelling. Establish your lodging budget before searching for choices. Remember that costs can change depending on the area and the season. In addition to possibly providing greater social chances for tourists, hostels are frequently less expensive than hotels.

Ask the hotel directly about rates and availability if you're interested in a particular hotel. You might be able to bargain for a lower price or request more services by getting in touch with them personally.

Request recommendations: Consult with friends, family members, or acquaintances who have travelled to Romania in the past for advice on hotels and hostels. Based on their experiences, they may be able to offer insightful advice about the finest places to stay.

Advance reservations are typically recommended, especially during the busiest travel times. This will guarantee that you have a place to stay and that you get the greatest deals. Making a reservation in advance also allows you more time to look up and evaluate other housing possibilities.

Check the cancellation regulations when making your reservation for lodging. If you need to cancel your reservation, this will make it easier for you to comprehend the terms and restrictions. While some hotels may impose a cancellation fee, others might provide a full refund.

Look for hidden costs: Carefully read the terms and conditions before making a reservation for lodging. For extra services like parking, resort fees, or cleaning costs, some hotels may charge a hidden fee. Before making a reservation for lodging, be sure you are aware of all the costs.

Safety: When travelling, safety should always come first. Pick accommodations that are located in secure areas. Look for hotels with security features like CCTV cameras, security personnel, and electronic key cards.

Tip #19: Guide to booking accommodations in Romania

One of the most crucial things you must do while organising a vacation to Romania is make reservations for your lodging. This manual will help you through the process of locating and reserving lodging in Romania.

Decide on a budget.

It's crucial to decide your budget before browsing for hotels. Knowing how much you can pay can help you narrow down the variety of lodging alternatives available in Romania, which vary from elegant hotels to hostels that are affordable. Do some research to get a feel of what you might anticipate to pay, keeping in mind that rates vary depending on the region and time of year.

Choose the place you desire.

There are many stunning and interesting places in Romania, from the Transylvania region with its enchanting ancient cities and castles to the Black Sea coast with its beaches and resorts. Based on your hobbies and travel schedule, choose the neighbourhood you want to stay in. Search for lodging in smaller towns or villages if you're planning to explore the countryside of Romania. You could wish to stay in Bucharest or another Romanian city if you're more interested in the nightlife and urban culture.

Examine the available accommodations.

In Romania, lodging options are plentiful and diverse, ranging from hotels and hostels to guesthouses, flats, and villas. The type of lodgings that best meet your needs and tastes should be taken into account. A hostel or guesthouse might be a suitable choice if you're on a tight budget and don't mind sharing a room. A villa or apartment can be a better option if you value privacy and space more.

Review articles

Once you've whittled down your choices, read traveller reviews to get a feel for what to anticipate. You can learn more about the calibre of lodgings and other tourists' experiences by reading reviews posted by prior guests on websites like Booking.com, TripAdvisor, and Expedia.

Look into the facilities

Aspects like WiFi, air conditioning, breakfast, and parking should all be considered while making a reservation. If a pool or fitness centre are important to you, some lodgings might offer them as extra facilities.

Purchase in advance

Last but not least, planning beforehand is crucial, especially if you're visiting during a busy tourist period. You will have somewhere to stay as a result, and you might even get a deal on lodging. Additionally, certain lodgings could provide discounts for early reservations.

Chapter 6. Dining And Nightlife

Dining and nightlife are the different options for food and entertainment that are offered in the evening and at night. Fast food joints, gourmet dining establishments, cafes, and food markets are just a few of the possibilities for dining. These places serve a variety of foods to satisfy a variety of palates and dietary needs.

The term "nightlife," on the other hand, describes the leisure activities that are offered after the sun goes down. This can apply to theatres, live music venues, taverns, and clubs. Nightlife establishments provide a variety of entertainment alternatives for patrons to take advantage of, including musical performances, dancing, and mingling.

Dining out is frequently enjoyed before or after participating in nocturnal entertainment, therefore the two frequently go hand in hand. Cities all around the world are renowned for their exciting eating and nightlife scenes, which draw both visitors and locals. Cities' nightlife environments can vary widely from one another; some are renowned for their hip pubs and clubs, while others are noted for their Michelin-starred eateries.

Tip #20: Overview of Romania's cuisine culinary traditions

The numerous cultural influences and lengthy history of Romania are reflected in its cuisine. Romania, which is located at the intersection of Central and Eastern Europe, has experienced invasions and control from a number of distinct ethnic groups, including the Romans, Turks, Hungarians, and Austrians. Romanian food has adopted components from these many civilizations as a result, while still retaining its own unique personality.

The utilisation of fresh, regional ingredients is one of what makes Romanian food distinctive. Many cuisines include vegetables and herbs that are sourced from nearby forests or gardens. Additionally, meat plays a significant role in Romanian cuisine, with pork being the most popular variety. Many rural communities continue to use traditional preparation techniques including smoking and curing.

Sarmale, or basically stuffed cabbage rolls, is one of the most well-liked foods in Romania. The rolls are frequently served with sour cream and polenta, and their customary filling is ground pork, rice, and seasonings. A different well-liked meal is mici, which are little sausages cooked from a combination of ground beef and pig and spiced with garlic and other ingredients.

There are numerous variations of soup, which is a significant component of Romanian cuisine. One of the most well-known is ciorbă, a sour soup composed with vegetables, meat, and a souring agent like vinegar or sour cream. Similar to many other Eastern European nations, Romania is a favourite place to eat borscht, a beet soup.

In addition to these basics, Romanian cuisine offers a wide selection of pastries and desserts. The most well-known of these is cozonac, a sweet bread made with raisins, almonds, and occasionally chocolate. Another well-liked sweet is called papanasi, and it consists of fried dough that has been covered with jam and sour cream.

Wine, beer, and a plum-based liquor known as tuica are among the alcoholic drinks that are used in Romanian cuisine. In Romania, winemaking has a rich history that dates back to the Roman era. Romanian wines are renowned for their complexity and depth of taste and the nation is home to numerous distinct grape varieties.

Rural areas of Romania continue to create and eat a number of traditional Romanian meals, but the nation's metropolitan population has increasingly embraced international cuisine. Numerous major towns around the world are home to Romanian eateries that serve traditional fare like ciorbă, sarmale, and mici.

With the help of numerous chefs who use traditional ingredients and culinary methods, Romanian cuisine has recently become well-known on a global scale. Food festivals and other culinary events are also increasing in frequency in Romania, displaying the nation's rich culinary traditions to a larger audience.

The country's history and cultural influences are largely reflected in the rich and diverse cuisine of Romania. It provides a distinctive and mouthwatering culinary experience with a focus on local, fresh products and traditional preparation techniques. There is something to savour in the world of Romanian food for everyone, whether you prefer sweet pastries or robust meat meals.

Tip #21: Guide to finding the best restaurants and cafes in Romania

The rich history and numerous cultural influences of Romania are reflected in its cuisine. Romania, which is located at the intersection of Central and Eastern Europe, has experienced invasions and control from a variety of peoples, including the Romans, Turks, Hungarians, and Austrians. As a result, while retaining its own unique personality, Romanian food has adopted components from these many cultures.

The utilisation of fresh, regional ingredients is one of the distinctive aspects of Romanian cuisine.

Vegetables and herbs from gardens or foraged from nearby forests are used in numerous cuisines. The most popular sort of meat in Romanian cuisine is pig, which is also a significant ingredient. In many rural areas, traditional preparation techniques including smoking and curing are still in use.

Sarmale, which is essentially stuffed cabbage rolls, is one of the most well-liked foods in Romania. The rolls are frequently served with sour cream and polenta, and their customary filling includes ground pork, rice, and spices. Another well-liked meal is mici, which are little sausages cooked from a combination of ground beef and pig and spiced with garlic and other ingredients.

There are many distinct variations of soup, which is a significant component of Romanian cuisine. Ciorbă, a sour soup composed with vegetables, meat, and a souring ingredient like vinegar or sour cream, is one of the most well-liked varieties. As in many other Eastern European nations, borscht, a beet soup, is a preferred cuisine in Romania.

Romanian cuisine also includes a variety of desserts and pastries in addition to these classics. One of the most well-known is cozonac, a sweet bread baked with raisins, almonds, and occasionally chocolate.

Another well-known delicacy is papanasi, which consists of fried dough covered with jam and sour cream.

Wine, beer, and a plum-based spirit known as tuica are among the alcoholic beverages that are used in Romanian cuisine. Romania has a lengthy history of wine production that dates back to the Roman era. Numerous distinct grape varieties may be found throughout the nation, and Romanian wines are renowned for their complexity and depth of flavour.

Although the country's urban population has adopted foreign cuisine, many traditional Romanian meals are still cooked and consumed in rural areas. Numerous major towns around the world have Romanian eateries that provide traditional meals as well as specialties like mici, sarmale, and ciorbă.

With the help of numerous chefs who use traditional ingredients and culinary methods, Romanian cuisine has recently attracted attention on a global scale. Food festivals and other culinary events are becoming more popular in Romania, exhibiting the nation's rich culinary traditions to a larger audience.

Overall, Romanian cuisine is a rich and diverse representation of the nation's history and cultural influences. It offers a distinctive and mouthwatering culinary experience with a focus on locally produced, fresh ingredients. Everyone can find something they like in the realm of Romanian food, whether they prefer savoury meat meals or sweet desserts.

Tip #22: Suggestions for experiencing romania's nightlife scene

The nightlife in Romania has plenty to offer for everyone, from subterranean clubs to hip bars and upscale eateries. The nightlife scene in Romania can be experienced in a few different ways, which we will discuss in this post.

Journey to Bucharest

One of the liveliest and most energetic cities in Europe is Bucharest, which serves as the nation's capital. Some of the nightclubs, bars, and restaurants there are among the most recognizable in the nation. Electronic music, hip-hop, jazz, and live music are all featured in the city's diversified nightlife culture, which has something for everyone.

Control, one of Bucharest's most well-known clubs, features some of the top DJs in the city's electronic music scene, both from abroad and from Romania. The venue is ideal for dancing the night away because of its cutting-edge sound system and contemporary decor. In Bucharest, prominent clubs including Kristal Glam Club, Bamboo, and Club A are also present.

Study Cluj-Napoca

The second-largest city in România is Cluj-Napoca, which is renowned for its thriving student community and exciting nightlife scene. There are several taverns, pubs, and clubs in the city that may accommodate a variety of interests and preferences. Midi Club, well-known for its electronic music scene, and Diesel Club, which has some of the top live music artists in the city, are two of Cluj-Napoca's most well-liked nightclubs.

Observe the Black Sea Coast.

The Black Sea Coast is the place to go if you're seeking for a one-of-a-kind and spectacular nightlife experience. The best beach clubs, pubs, and eateries in Romania are located along the coast, where you can dance the night away and take in the breathtaking views of the water. The best beach clubs along the Black Sea Coast include the Fratelli Beach & Club, Loft Mamaia, and Ego Club.

Check out Brasov

In the middle of Romania, in the delightful mediaeval town of Brasov, which is renowned for both its beautiful architecture and long history. Aside from having some of the top bars and restaurants in the nation, the town also has a vibrant and varied nightlife. Les Elephants Bistro Bar, which serves delectable cocktails and has a warm and friendly ambiance, and Astra Library Bar, which is housed in a historic library and has a distinctive and exquisite design, are two of the most well-liked bars in Brasov.

Discover the Local Drinks

The native libations must be sampled during any visit to Romania's nightlife scene. In bars and restaurants all throughout Romania, you may choose from a large selection of mouthwatering and top-notch wines. The strong plum brandy known as Tuica is another well-liked beverage in Romania. It is often consumed as an aperitif or digestif. The fruit brandy Palinka and the well-liked regional brew Ursus are other popular beverages in Romania.

Chapter 7. Attractions And Activities

Tip #23: Romania's top tourist attractions

The greatest tourist destinations in Romania have plenty to offer everyone, from historic fortifications and mediaeval towns to spectacular mountain vistas and charming beach towns. We'll look at a few of Romania's most well-liked tourist attractions in this article.

Castle Bran

One of Romania's most well-known sites is Bran Castle, which is situated in the charming Transylvania region. This majestic fortification, which originates to the 14th century, is frequently linked to the Dracula legend. The castle is a must-see attraction for tourists to Romania because of its stunning Gothic architecture and picturesque mountain setting.

Castle Peles

Peles Castle, which is situated in the town of Sinaia, is another well-known castle in Romania. Built in the late 19th century, this lovely castle was the Romanian royal family's summer retreat until 1947. One of the most beautiful castles in Europe, the castle is distinguished by its eclectic design and stunning interior.

Sighişoara

A stunning mediaeval city called Sighisoara can be found right in the middle of Transylvania. The city's historical district, which is a UNESCO World Heritage Site, is home to a lovely assortment of vibrant buildings, winding streets, and breathtaking Gothic architecture. The birthplace of Vlad the Impaler, the figurehead for Bram Stoker's Dracula, is another notable fact about the city.

Brasov

Brasov is a picturesque city in central Romania's Carpathian Mountains. The magnificent Black Church, one of the largest Gothic churches in Eastern Europe, is among the magnificent collection of mediaeval structures found in the city's lovely old town. With surrounding ski areas, hiking routes, and breathtaking mountain scenery, Brasov is also a fantastic location for outdoor enthusiasts.

Delta du Danube

Eastern Romania is home to the Danube Delta, a sizable wetland region where the Danube River empties into the Black Sea. The delta is a haven for bird lovers since it is home to an incredible variety of wildlife, including over 300 species of birds. With the help of a boat, visitors can cruise the delta's numerous canals and waterways in search of endangered species including pelicans, cormorants, and eagles.

Bucovina's Painted Monasteries

Northeastern Romania is home to the magnificent Orthodox monasteries known as The Painted Monasteries of Bucovina. The monasteries have vibrant murals and frescoes that portray episodes from the Bible and saints' lives. The monasteries are regarded as some of the most significant specimens of Byzantine art in Europe and are a UNESCO World Heritage Site.

Cluj-Napoca

A thriving university town in the centre of Transylvania is Cluj-Napoca. Beautiful architecture, a thriving cultural scene, and a fun nightlife are some of the city's most well-known features. Visitors can enjoy the city's numerous eateries, pubs, and cafes or visit the numerous museums, galleries, and historic sites.

Castle Corvin

The city of Hunedoara is home to the remarkable mediaeval stronghold known as Corvin Castle. The castle, which was built in the fifteenth century, has outstanding Gothic architecture, including great towers, high walls, and lovely courtyards. The castle, which is frequently cited as one of Europe's most beautiful, is a must-visit location for tourists to Romania.

The Merry Graveyard

In the village of Sapanta, in the northern part of Romania, there is a special place called The Merry Cemetery. The cemetery is renowned for its bright and amusing wooden crosses that include hand-carved illustrations and hilarious epitaphs. The cemetery serves as both a celebration of life and a warning against taking dying too seriously.

Highway Transfagarasan

Central Romania's Carpathian Mountains are traversed by the breathtaking Transfagarasan Highway, a mountain route. The road was constructed in the 1970s as a vital military route and is today one of Europe's most beautiful drives. The road passes through spectacular alpine scenery, through glacial lakes and waterfalls, and provides breath-taking vistas from several of its viewpoint sites.

Bucharest

Romania's capital, Bucharest, is a thriving centre of culture, history, and contemporary life. Beautiful architecture, a buzzing nightlife, and top-notch museums and galleries are some of the city's most well-known features. Visitors can discover the city's numerous treasures, including the stunning

Stavropoleos Monastery, one of the most striking specimens of Romanian Orthodox architecture, and the Palace of the Parliament, the largest administrative structure in the world.

Lake Balea
A stunning glacial lake called Balea Lake may be found in central Romania's Fagaras Mountains. A beautiful cable car trip will take you to the lake, which provides breathtaking views of the surrounding alpine landscape. Hiking around the lake, fishing, and other outdoor pursuits are all available to visitors

Brasov Castle
On a hilltop overlooking the city of Brasov, the well-preserved mediaeval fortification known as the Brasov fortification may be found. The fortress, which was constructed in the fourteenth century, served as a crucial defensive bastion for the area. Visitors can stroll through the fortress's several walls and towers while taking in the breathtaking views of the surrounding countryside.

National Museum of Peles
The beautiful Peles National Museum is housed in Sinaia's Peles Castle. The museum displays the rich cultural legacy of Romania through an

extraordinary collection of artwork, furniture, and decorative items. The many rooms of the castle are open for exploration, and guests can see the exquisite architecture and style.

Brasov, Poiana

Central Romania's Carpathian Mountains are home to the well-known ski resort of Poiana Brasov. Along with other winter sports like sledding and ice skating, the resort offers a large variety of skiing and snowboarding activities. Visitors can engage in outdoor activities including hiking and mountain biking during the summer.

Tip #24: Historical sites, natural wonders

Numerous historical sites and natural wonders in this stunning nation draw tourists from all over the world. The most significant historical landmarks and natural wonders in Romania will be covered in this essay.

Historic Places

Romania is a nation with a lengthy and fascinating history that has been shaped over the years by a wide variety of cultures. There are many historical sites in the nation, including castles, churches, and fortified cities. The most notable ones are listed below:

Castle Bran

One of Romania's most well-known castles, Bran Castle is well-known for its connection to the Count Dracula legend. This magnificent castle was constructed in the 14th century as a stronghold to ward off Ottoman incursions and is situated in the Carpathian Mountains. Today, it serves as a museum and draws countless tourists each year.

Castle Corvin

The city of Hunedoara is home to Corvin Castle, one of the biggest castles in all of Europe. It is a magnificent specimen of Gothic architecture that dates back to the 14th century. Throughout its history, the castle has served as a home, a military outpost, and a jail.

Citadel of Sighişoara

The fortified city of Sighisoara in Transylvania is one of Europe's best-preserved mediaeval citadels. It was constructed in the 12th century and is renowned for its brightly coloured homes, cobblestone lanes, and formidable walls. Additionally, Vlad the Impaler, the model for Dracula in Bram Stoker's novel Dracula, was born in this city.

The Bucovina Painted Monasteries

Northern Romania is home to a group of UNESCO World Heritage Sites known as The Painted Monasteries of Bucovina. Their beautiful paintings and murals, which were painted in the 15th and 16th centuries, are renowned worldwide. The monasteries are tucked away in the countryside, surrounded by stunning scenery.

Natural marvels

Some of Europe's most stunning natural treasures may be found in Romania. The nation is a haven for environment lovers, with everything from the rough Carpathian Mountains to the undulating hills of Transylvania. Here are a few of Romania's most renowned natural wonders:

Delta of the Danube

A UNESCO World Heritage Site, the Danube Delta is one of the biggest and most biodiverse wetlands in the world. More than 5,500 different plant and animal species may be found there, and it is situated in the eastern region of the nation. The delta can be toured on foot, by boat, or by kayak.

The Carpathian Range

The breathtaking Carpathian Mountain range can be found in Romania and numerous other Eastern European nations. Numerous hiking paths, ski areas, and wildlife refuges can be found there. Numerous traditional villages can be found in the mountains, providing a look into Romanian rural life.

The Turda Mine for Salt

In Transylvania, there is a distinctive underground attraction called the Turda Salt Mine. In the 17th century, it was used as a salt mine; in 1992, it was transformed into a tourist destination. The mine's underground chambers, which contain lakes below ground and stalactites, are open to visitors.

Highway Transfagarasan

A magnificent mountain route that travels through the Carpathian Mountains is called the Transfagarasan Highway. It is renowned for its spectacular views, hairpin curves, and gorgeous scenery. The route is a well-liked location for road excursions and motorbike tours even though it is only open from June to October.

Tip #25: Suggestions for outdoor activities and adventure sports

If you enjoy the outdoors or are an adrenaline junkie, Romania has something for you. Here are some ideas for outdoor pursuits and adventure sports in Romania, from trekking in the Carpathian Mountains to white-water rafting on the Danube.

The Carpathian Mountains hiking

Many parts of Romania are covered by the Carpathian Mountains, which provide some of the best trekking options in the continent. There are paths for people of various fitness levels and experience levels, ranging from short strolls to strenuous multi day excursions. The Fagaras Mountains, Retezat Mountains, and Bucegi Mountains are a few of the most well-liked hiking locations. One of the most beautiful journeys in the world is the Transfagarasan Highway, which passes through the Fagaras Mountains.

Snowboarding and skiing

Poiana Brasov, Sinaia, and Predeal are just a few of the ski resorts in Romania that provide a variety of slopes for skiers and snowboarders of all skill levels. In Romania, the ski season normally lasts from December to March, with January and February offering the finest skiing. The Carpathians offer options for cross-country skiing and snowshoeing in addition to downhill skiing.

Rafting across rapids

Some of the best white-water rafting in Europe can be found on the Danube River, which flows through Romania. There are numerous businesses that provide guided rafting experiences, ranging from straightforward excursions suitable for families to more difficult rapids for seasoned rafters. The Bicaz Gorge, the Jiu River, and the Olt River are a few of the most well-liked rafting locations.

A rock climb

Rock climbing is becoming increasingly popular in Romania, where there are numerous climbing locations. The Piatra Craiului Mountains, the Rarau Mountains, and the Turda Gorge are a few of the most well-known locations. Numerous indoor climbing gyms may be found in large towns like Bucharest and Cluj-Napoca.

There is a vast network of bicycle lanes and routes in Romania, from family-friendly, easy rides to more difficult mountain bike trails. The Danube Cycle Path, which follows the Danube River, and the Transfagarasan Highway, which is well-liked by road cyclists, are two of the most well-travelled routes. Numerous bike rental businesses also provide self-directed and guided outings.

The Scarisoara Ice Cave, the Bears' Cave, and the Pestera Ursilor Cave are just a few of the impressive and enormous caves found in Romania. Many of these caves offer unique opportunities to explore underground lakes, stalactites, and stalagmites and many of them offer guided tours.

Paragliding

There are many places to paraglide in Romania, including the Carpathian Mountains and the port city of Constanta. While more seasoned paragliders can use the thermals and mountain breezes to go great distances, tandem flights are offered for beginners.

Equestrian riding

Horseback riding has a long history in Romania, and many businesses offer escorted tours through the countryside on horses. The Danube Delta, the Bucegi Mountains, and the Maramures region are a few of the most well-liked vacation spots.

Tip #26: Tips for experiencing Romania's festivals and other cultural events

With numerous festivals and cultural events occurring all year long, Romania is a nation rich in history and culture. In Romania, there is always something happening, from music festivals to traditional holidays. The following advice will help you get the most out of your time at Romania's festivals and cultural events.

In advance

Look up the festivals and cultural events scheduled during your visit to Romania before you leave. You can use this information to arrange your schedule and make sure you don't skip any important events. To avoid disappointment, make sure to purchase your tickets in advance for the many festivals and cultural events that require them.

Consider your attire.

It's crucial to dress correctly for the weather because many of Romania's festivals and cultural events take place outside. Bring sunscreen, a hat, and light clothing in the summer because it can get very hot. Make careful you pack layers and warm clothing for the winter because it can get below freezing.

Examine the local cuisine

Attending festivals and other cultural events in Romania and getting to experience the local food is one of the nicest parts. There is always wonderful food to try, whether it be ethnic or street food. A must-try is the high-quality, locally-produced wine and beer.

Learn some fundamental Romanian

Even if many Romanians are English speakers, it's a good idea to learn some fundamental Romanian words before going to festivals and other cultural events. This will enable you to interact with people and demonstrate your appreciation for their way of life.

Honour regional traditions

When visiting festivals and cultural events, remember that Romanians take pride in their traditions and customs. For instance, it is crucial to dress modestly and behave with respect when attending religious processions and rituals during festivals and other cultural events.

Plan ahead for crowds.

Numerous Romanian festivals and cultural events enjoy enormous popularity and draw tens of thousands of tourists from all over the world. Especially during well-attended events like the Sighisoara Medieval Festival and the Braşov Christmas Market, be ready for enormous crowds. Be patient when negotiating through crowds and arrive early to obtain a good place.

Be cautious.

When visiting festivals and cultural events in Romania, as with any major event, it's crucial to exercise caution. Keep your valuables close by, and always be mindful of your surroundings. If you're going to an event in a remote place with few medical services, be ready for it and take all required precautions, such as taking bug repellent and first aid materials.

Take part in the culture.

Finally, if you want to truly appreciate Romania's festivals and cultural events, you need immerse yourself in the community. engage in regional customs and traditions, observe traditional dances and performances, and engage in traditional ceremonies and processions. In addition to improving your experience, this will demonstrate respect for the local way of life.

Chapter 8. Practical Information

Tip #27: Currency and banking information

The Romanian leu (RON), the currency of Romania, is the seventh most populous member state of the European Union. The currency and banking information for Romania will be covered in this page.

The Romanian Leu:

The official currency of Romania is the Romanian leu, abbreviated as RON. 100 bani are equal to one leu. A dollar is currently worth around 4.16 RON at the current exchange rate of the Romanian leu, which is about 0.24 US dollars.

Since its debut in 1867, the Romanian leu has experienced a number of modifications. The most recent modification occurred in 2005 when the new leu (RON) was created to replace the old leu (ROL) at a ratio of 10,000 old lei to one new leu.

Coins and banknotes in the new leu (RON) are readily accessible. Along with 1 and 5 lei, coins come in denominations of 1, 5, 10, and 50 bani. Banknotes come in 1, 5, 10, 50, 100, 200, and 500 lei denominations. The images on the banknotes include well-known Romanian figures and locations, including the King Carol I statue, the Peles Castle, and the Palace of the Parliament.

Romania's banking sector:

A comprehensive range of services are provided to both individuals and businesses by Romania's well-developed banking industry. Banca Transilvania, Raiffeisen Bank, BCR, BRD - Groupe Société Générale, and ING Bank are just a few of the domestic and foreign banks that are active in the nation.

It's simple to open a bank account in Romania, whether you do it online or in person at a bank branch. You will want a legitimate form of identity, like a passport or national ID card, as well as evidence of your address, such a utility bill or rental agreement, in order to create a bank account.

In Romania, the majority of banks provide a variety of banking services, such as checking and savings accounts, credit and debit cards, loans, mortgages, and insurance products. The ability to manage accounts, transfer money, pay bills, and examine transactions via a computer or mobile device is also commonly available thanks to online banking.

Some banks in Romania provide specialised services in addition to conventional banking ones, including wealth management, financial advice, and foreign exchange. Additionally, there are a number of fintech businesses functioning in the nation that provide cutting-edge options for lending, investing, and making payments.

Romania's banking industry is, in general, up to date, effective, and competitive, providing a wide range of services to clients at affordable prices. You may probably discover a banking solution in Romania that meets your needs, whether you're a person or a corporation.

Tip #28: Emergency contact numbers and important health and safety tips

One should be aware of a number of crucial emergency contact numbers in Romania. These numbers should be kept in mind in case of an emergency since they may help save your life or the life of a loved one.

First off, in case of an emergency, dial 112. You can call this number in the event of any emergency, including those involving the police, fires, or medical conditions. When dialling 112, it's crucial to maintain composure and provide the operator as much information as you can.

You can also dial 961 if you need medical assistance. You can dial this number to be connected to an ambulance in case of a medical emergency. It is crucial to remember that Romania's ambulances are run by the government and are provided at no cost.

A visitor to Romania should be aware of a number of crucial health and safety recommendations in addition to these emergency numbers. Using these suggestions can help you stay secure and healthy throughout your journey.

One of the most crucial guidelines is to only consume bottled water. Although drinking Romanian tap water is typically safe, it is always preferable to err on the side of caution and only use bottled water. Before buying the bottle, make sure the seal is still intact because there have been instances of fake bottled water being sold in the past.

Understanding the local meteorological conditions is also crucial. It's crucial to pack for the season because Romania has frigid winters and scorching summers. Make sure to pack warm clothing throughout the winter because temperatures can fall below freezing. As temperatures might get above 40 degrees Celsius in the summer, remember to wear sunscreen and drink plenty of water.

It's crucial to be knowledgeable of Romanian driving regulations if you intend to drive there. Highways typically have a 130 km/h speed limit, and driving under the influence of alcohol carries severe penalties. Additionally, it is crucial to always keep your automobile locked because car theft is a major issue in Romania.

It's crucial to always be aware of your surroundings when it comes to personal safety. Avoid going for a nighttime solo walk, and use public transit with caution. Keep your valuables close by, and stay away from carrying a lot of cash with you.

Prior to flying to Romania, it is crucial to ensure that you are up to date on all of your immunizations in terms of your health. Hepatitis A and B, typhoid, and rabies are just a few of the diseases that are thought to pose a risk to the nation. To ensure that you are properly immunised, consult your doctor before travelling to Romania.

Finally, it's critical to understand Romanian culture and customs before visiting. It is crucial to respect the locals' customs and traditions because the nation has a rich history and culture. Before your travel, brush up on your Romanian and make an attempt to become a part of the community.

Tip #29: Guide to transportation options within Romania

Everyone has a choice, whether they are searching for comfort, affordability, or a chance to take in the country's breathtaking beauty. We'll give you a rundown of your Romanian transportation alternatives in this article.

Romania has a number of international airports, some of which are in the country's largest cities, including Bucharest, Cluj-Napoca, Timişoara, Iasi, and Constanta. The biggest and busiest airport in

Romania is Bucharest Henri Coanda International Airport, which serves major European cities as well as several Middle Eastern and North American locations. Numerous domestic and foreign destinations are served by flights from other airports.

Taking the Train

There are several transportation options that are both inexpensive and practical available on Romania's enormous rail network. The primary operator is the state-owned CFR (Romanian Railways), which runs trains linking Romania's important cities and towns. In accordance with their speed and facilities, the trains are divided into a number of classes, including InterCity, Regio, and Accelerate. Regio and Accelerate trains are slower but provide more reasonable rates, whereas InterCity trains offer faster and more comfortable travel. The train system is dependable, and the trip offers a great chance to discover Romania's beautiful scenery.

The Bus

Buses provide connections between small villages and cities and are a well-liked mode of transportation in Romania. Bus services are run by a number of businesses, like FlixBus, and they provide convenient and economical transport options. The buses have onboard facilities, reclining seats, and air conditioning. For individuals who prefer to visit smaller towns or explore rural areas that might not be accessible by rail, using the bus is a terrific option.

Rent a Car

If you want to see Romania at your own leisure, renting a car is a fantastic alternative. In Romania, a number of car rental firms, including Hertz, Avis, and Europcar, are in business and provide a vast selection of vehicles at affordable rates. Driving in Romania, however, can be difficult because of the nation's road infrastructure, which in some places is not always well-maintained.

Taxi :Taxis are generally accessible and may be found in Romania's major cities and municipalities. Taxi fares are reasonable, and the drivers are frequently dependable and kind. However, it's crucial to use authorised taxis to prevent fraud and overcharging.

Metro

One of the most effective and cost-effective modes of transportation in the city is the metro system in Bucharest. There are four lines in the metro system, which serves the majority of the city's key areas. It is a good alternative for commuters and tourists because the metro system is dependable and open from early in the morning until late at night.

Trolleybuses and trams

In Romania, notably in cities like Bucharest and Cluj-Napoca, trams and trolleybuses are other widely used modes of transportation. Regular services connecting various parts of the city are provided by the systems, which are both easy and economical.

In Romania, especially in major cities like Bucharest and Cluj-Napoca, cycling is becoming a more and more common form of transportation. In these locations, a number of bike-sharing systems are in operation, offering visitors and locals inexpensive and eco-friendly transportation choices.

Chapter 9. Language And Culture

Tip #30: Overview of Romania's language and cultural traditions

Romanian is the official language of the country; it is a Romance language that developed from Latin. There are more than 19 million people living in Romania, and the majority of them are first-language Romanian speakers. Hungarian,

German, and Romani speakers are substantial minority groups, though.

The grammar of Romanian is renowned for being intricate, utilising both definite and indefinite articles, declensions, and verb conjugations. Additionally, it has a large lexicon that incorporates many words from Latin, Greek, Slavic, and other languages. The Romanian alphabet has 31 letters total, including the unusual letter ă, which sounds like the English letter "uh."

The geography, religion, and customs of Romania, as well as a long history of invasions and other influences, have all influenced its culture. The Carpathian Mountains, which cut through the country's middle, and the Danube River, which serves as its southern border, are what define its geography. With influences from nearby nations like Hungary, Serbia, Bulgaria, and Ukraine, this has produced a diverse blend of cultures and traditions.

The folk traditions of Romania, which include music, dance, and costume, are among its most distinguishing features. The cimbalom, a hammered dulcimer, and the pan flute are common instruments used to perform folk music, which is a significant component of Romanian culture. Folk dances from Romania are very well-liked, and they are frequently performed while wearing regionally specific traditional attire.

The cultural traditions of the nation provide an essential component of Romanian food. Hearty stews, grilled meats, and vegetable dishes make up its staple menu. Traditional alcoholic drinks like palinca, a sort of brandy, and tuica, a plum brandy, are frequently served as an accompaniment. Sarmale, which are cabbage rolls stuffed with rice and meat, and mici, which are rolls of grilled minced meat, are both well-liked delicacies.

With the bulk of the populace being Eastern Orthodox Christians, religion is a significant component in Romanian culture as well. Romanian art, literature, and architecture all show the profound impact that Orthodox Christianity has had on the nation's culture. Significant Protestant and Catholic minorities as well as smaller Jewish and Muslim populations also exist in Romania.

Numerous well-known authors and poets, such Mihai Eminescu and Ion Creanga, are part of Romania's rich literary legacy. The lengthy history of foreign rule and cultural interchange in Romania has influenced the literature, which frequently examines issues of identity, history, and nationalism. With recent international award wins for movies like The Death of Mr. Lazarescu and 4 Months, 3 Weeks and 2 Days, Romanian cinema has also become more well-known.

Romania is renowned for its stunning Orthodox churches, many of which have elaborate paintings and icons. Many stunning castles and palaces can be found throughout the nation, including the well-known Bran Castle, which is credited with serving as the model for Dracula in Bram Stoker's novel.

Tip #31: Tips for interacting with locals and understanding Romanian customs and etiquette

Understanding local customs and manners is crucial for making the most of your trip to Romania. The following advice will help you communicate with people in Romania and learn about their traditions.

Gain some Romanian language skills

Although English is widely spoken in Romania, the official language is Romanian, and visitors are usually grateful when they make an effort to speak a little bit of Romanian. "Bună ziua" (hello), "mulțumesc" (thank you), and "la revedere" (goodbye) are a few simple expressions to learn. Additionally, you can pick up certain idioms for shopping, requesting directions, and placing an order for meals.

Be well attired.

Romanians take care in their appearance and appreciate when tourists are well-groomed and wear conservative clothing. When visiting holy locations, especially, stay out of any suggestive or revealing apparel. A general expression of respect for the local culture is to dress modestly and conservatively.

Shake hands to welcome others.

Shaking hands is traditional when meeting someone for the first time. Smiling and saying "bună ziua" (hello) while maintaining eye contact. Use of titles and surnames is appropriate in more formal settings, such as business meetings or government functions.

Being on time

The punctuality of others is something that Romanians cherish. Calling in advance to let the person know you'll be late is polite. It's common for the host to be a few minutes late when you've been invited to someone's house, though.

Regard seniors with respect.
Romanian culture strongly values respect for the elderly. Never use a younger person's title or last name while you are around an older one. After their last name, use "doamnă" (Mrs.) or "domnul" (Mr.). When an elderly person enters the room, one should also stand up.

Steer clear of delicate subjects
Despite being sensitive on occasion, Romanians are proud of their nation and their past. If your local host doesn't start the conversation, stay away from topics like politics, religion, and Romania's time under communism.

Make good use of the tools.
Use utensils correctly when you're eating. Left hand holds the fork, while the right hand holds the knife. While you're eating, avoid resting your elbows on

the table, and always keep your hands out in front of you.

Proposal to pay
It's normal to bring a little present, like flowers or chocolates, or to offer to pay for dinner when you're asked to go to someone's home for a meal. The host should be respected if they decline your offer, though.

Observe regional traditions
Numerous national traditions are only practised in Romania. When visiting someone's home, for instance, it's normal to offer a modest gift. It's also customary to take off your shoes before entering a home. Don't be hesitant to ask questions if you have any doubts and respect the norms and traditions of the area.

Savour the regional fare
The food is tasty and varied in Romania. Eat some of the regional specialties including sarmale (stuffed cabbage rolls), mici (grilled minced beef buns), and ciorbă (sour soup). Also great and worth trying is Romanian wine.

Tip #32: Suggestions for learning more about romania's history and culture

Throughout its history, Romania has been affected by a wide range of cultures. The history and culture of Romania can be intriguing and pleasant to learn about. Here are some ideas on how to learn more about the history and culture of Romania:

Observe museums

The history and culture of Romania can be studied in great detail at museums. Throughout the nation, there are numerous museums that display various facets of Romania's past and present. Anyone interested in learning about the history of Romania must visit the National Museum of Romanian History in Bucharest. The museum has displays covering prehistoric, Dacian, Roman, mediaeval, and modern history of Romania. The National Museum of Art of Romania and the Museum of the Romanian Peasant are two further noteworthy museums.

Visit historical locations

Numerous historical landmarks in Romania provide a look into the nation's colourful past. The most well-known of these is without a doubt Bran Castle, also referred to as "Dracula's Castle." It is said that the Transylvanian castle served as the basis for Bram Stoker's well-known book. The painted monasteries of Bucovina, the fortified cathedrals of Transylvania, and the Roman ruins in Constanta are further historical locations well worth visiting.

Cultural activities to attend
Romania is renowned for having a thriving cultural scene, with numerous festivals and events occurring all year long. Taking part in these activities is a wonderful way to become more familiar with Romanian culture and customs. The Sibiu International Theatre Festival, the George Enescu Festival, and the Transylvania International Film Festival are a few well-known occasions.

Study books.
An excellent method to learn more about Romania is through reading books about its history and culture.

See motion pictures and documentaries
Another option to learn about the history and culture of Romania is to watch films and documentaries. The history of Romania, both ancient and modern, has been the subject of numerous movies and documentaries.

Take language classes.

Gaining a greater grasp of Romanian culture can be accomplished very well by learning the language. Although English is commonly spoken in Romania, knowing a little bit of the local language might help you interact with locals and appreciate the subtleties of their culture. There are numerous language schools offering classes to foreigners all around Romania, as well as a wealth of internet resources for learning Romanian.

Interact with residents

One of the finest methods to learn about Romanian culture is to interact with locals. Locals can provide ideas for places to visit and activities to do as well as insights into the country's customs and traditions. There are several methods to interact with locals, from participating in language exchange programs to staying with a local family through a homestay program.

Conclusion

In conclusion, Romania is a beautiful country with a long history and a variety of cultures. Romania has a lot to offer both tourists and locals, from its imposing castles and mediaeval cities to its breathtaking mountains and beaches. However, the nation still has to deal with issues like corruption and economic inequality that can impede its growth. Despite these difficulties, Romania is nonetheless an intriguing and distinctive location that is absolutely worth visiting. Everybody may find something to enjoy in Romania, regardless of their interests in nature, history, culture, or adventure.

Recap of what makes Romania a unique and exciting travel destination

Tourists have been drawn to Romania for years because it is a distinct and intriguing holiday destination. Romania, a country in southeast Europe, is home to enchanted landscapes, historic castles, charming towns, and energetic cities. Any travel enthusiast should go there because of its rich history, culture, and natural beauty.

To begin with, Romania is the country where Dracula's Castle, one of the most well-known sites in the world, is located. This castle, which may be found in the Transylvanian town of Bran, has come to represent the story of the ruthless vampire. In addition to its eerie legends, the castle is a magnificent example of Gothic architecture with its towers, turrets, and hidden tunnels. While discovering the history of the area, visitors can tour the castle's expansive halls, intricate staircases, and secret passageways.

Romania is home to a large number of other mediaeval strongholds and castles in addition to Dracula's Castle. The Corvin Castle, sometimes called Hunyadi Castle, which is situated in the town of Hunedoara, is one of the most impressive. The castle is a magnificent example of Gothic design and has a lengthy past that dates back more than 600 years. It has appeared in a number of motion pictures, notably the well-known horror film "Ghoulies III: Ghoulies Go to College."

Another significant draw for tourists is Romania's natural beauty. The nation is home to the Carpathian Mountains, which provide some of Europe's most breath-taking vistas. Popular activities in the area include hiking, skiing, and mountain climbing. Visitors from all over the world flock to see the Danube Delta, another natural wonder. The delta is a haven for birdwatchers as it is home to over 300 different species of birds.

Romania is renowned for its charming towns where it appears that time has stopped still. The village of Sighisoara, renowned for its intact mediaeval architecture, is one of the most well-known. The tale of Dracula was based on Vlad the Impaler, whose birthplace is in this town. Visitors can learn about the town's lengthy history while strolling through its cobblestone streets, colourful homes, and mediaeval fortress.

Romania offers a lot to people who enjoy dynamic cities. The nation's capital, Bucharest, is a thriving metropolis with a vibrant cultural scene. Along with some of the best nightlife in all of Europe, the city is home to various museums, galleries, and theatres. Another well-liked vacation spot is Cluj-Napoca, the second-largest city in Romania. It is also recognized for its stunning architecture, exciting music scene, and chic cafes and restaurants.

Romania is renowned for its delectable cuisine. Romanian cuisine includes sarmale (stuffed cabbage rolls), mici (rolls of grilled minced beef), and mamaliga (a sort of polenta). The nation is also well-known for its wine, which has been made for more than two thousand years. Visitors to Romania can explore the numerous vineyards and wineries there while tasting some of the greatest wines the nation has to offer.

Final tips and recommendations for visitors to Romania.

Here are some further advice and suggestions for travellers to Romania:

Although English is widely spoken in Romania, it is always appreciated when guests make an attempt to speak the local tongue. Making friends with the locals and leaving a positive impression can be achieved by learning some fundamental words and phrases like "hello" (salut), "thank you" (mulțumesc), and "goodbye" (la revedere).

Be conscious of your safety: Romania is often a safe country, but it's necessary to be aware of your surroundings and take measures when travelling anywhere. Keep your belongings safe, avoid walking alone at night in strange places.

Try the local food: Romanian cuisine is savoury and hearty, with influences from nearby Turkey and Hungary. Try some of the local specialties including papanasi (fried dough topped with jam and sour cream), mici (grilled minced beef buns), and sarmale (stuffed cabbage rolls).

While Bucharest and Cluj-Napoca are well-known tourist sites, there is much more to explore in Romania. Explore quaint mediaeval cities like Sighisoara and Brasov on a road trip across Transylvania, or visit the painted monasteries of Bucovina to learn more about the nation's extensive religious history.

A continental climate with four distinct seasons characterises Romania, therefore it's necessary to pack appropriately. Winters can be chilly and snowy, while summers can be hot and muggy. Check the weather forecast before you go and bring layers.

Respect local traditions and customs: Romania has a rich cultural legacy, so it's necessary to show consideration for them. When visiting holy sites, dress modestly, ask people's permission before taking their picture, and be mindful of regional greeting and gesture conventions.

Although Romania has a strong network of buses, trains, and cabs, it is still advisable to make transportation arrangements in advance, particularly if you are heading outside of the major cities. To travel more conveniently, think about renting a car or getting a driver.

Overall, Romania is a stunning and friendly nation with a lot to offer tourists. You may maximise your trip and make enduring memories by adhering to these advice and suggestions.

Printed in Great Britain
by Amazon

22218835R00079